Anonymous

Proceedings on the Opening of the Williamson Free School

of Mechanical Trades

Anonymous

Proceedings on the Opening of the Williamson Free School of Mechanical Trades

ISBN/EAN: 9783337286057

Printed in Europe, USA, Canada, Australia, Japan

Cover: Foto ©Paul-Georg Meister /pixelio.de

More available books at **www.hansebooks.com**

PROCEEDINGS

—ON THE—

OPENING

—OF THE—

WILLIAMSON FREE SCHOOL

—OF—

MECHANICAL TRADES.

October 31st, 1891.

The original Trustees appointed by the Foundation Deed of I. V. Williamson, dated December 1st, 1888, were:—

The present Board of Trustees consists of the following:—

CITY OFFICE:
ROOM No. 39, FORREST BUILDING,
119 South Fourth Street,
PHILADELPHIA.

OFFICERS, TEACHERS, ETC.

PRESIDENT,
JOHN M. SHRIGLEY.

SUPERINTENDENT,
ROBERT CRAWFORD.

TEACHER OF ENGLISH BRANCHES,
ABBIE A. EYRE.

TEACHER OF DRAWING AND PENMANSHIP,
H. S. BITTING.

TEACHER OF WOOD WORK,
FRANK GRANT.

HOUSEKEEPER,
EMMA STURR.

MATRONS,
SARAH M. RICHIE,   SUSAN S. CASSIN,   MRS. ALONZO DALTON.

ENGINEER,
ALONZO DALTON.

CLERK,
ALAN LEAMY.

Post-Office Address,

WILLIAMSON SCHOOL, DELAWARE CO., PA.

Railroad Station Address,

WILLIAMSON SCHOOL,

(Central Division P. W. & B. R. R.)

P. R. R.   DELAWARE CO., PA.

On the afternoon of Saturday, October 31st, 1891, a large and representative audience from the city of Philadelphia and its vicinity, in response to an invitation extended by the Trustees of the Williamson Free School of Mechanical Trades, assembled in the auditorium of the Main Administrative Building, at Williamson School, on the line of the West Chester and Philadelphia Railroad, near Media, Delaware County, Pennsylvania, to witness the exercises attending the formal opening of the school.

MR. SAMUEL B. HUEY, one of the Trustees, presided, and in opening said :

In a Christian land it is to be assumed that the blessing of God should be invoked upon the beginnings of educational institutions. In the foundation deed for this school Mr. Williamson said : '' I desire and direct that the moral and religious training of the scholars shall be properly looked after and cared for by the Trustees, but that there shall be no attempt by the Trustees at proselytism among the scholars, and no favoritism shown by the Trustees to any particular sect or creed.''

While this clause does not in terms indicate that our religious services shall not be conducted by clergymen, yet the Trustees have thought that its spirit would be best carried out by placing such services in the hands of laymen of approved Christian character. They have therefore invited Mr. B. B. Comegys, whose interest in all movements looking towards the education and care of the young is so well known, to lead us in an opening prayer asking for God's blessing upon the institution, interest in whose welfare has brought us together here this afternoon.

PRAYER BY B. B. COMEGYS.

Our Father, Who art in heaven, hallowed be Thy name. Thy kingdom come. Thy will be done on earth, as it is in heaven. Give us this day our daily bread. And forgive us our trespasses, as we forgive those who trespass against us. And lead us not into temptation, but deliver us from evil. For Thine is the kingdom, and the power, and the glory, forever, AMEN.

O God, Light of the hearts that see thee, and Life of the souls that love thee, and Strength of the thoughts that seek thee, from whom to be turned away is to fall, and to whom to turn is to rise, and in whom to abide is to stand fast forever; grant us now thy grace and blessing as we are assembled to call upon thy name.

We thank thee for the pleasant things about us to-day— for this great company assembled, and for their sympathy with us in the work which brings us together. We thank thee for putting it into the heart of the Founder of this school to set apart a portion of his wealth for so excellent a purpose; for the good thoughts he had for the young; for his desire that they should be instructed in useful trades; for the value he placed on liberal education and intelligent handicraft; for his choice of the men to whom this great work is committed; and for the wisdom and devotion they have manifested in the discharge of their responsible office.

And now we earnestly pray, O God, that thy blessing may rest upon this school. Give wisdom and grace in large measure continually to the Trustees, that they may always choose the best men and women to continue the work which under thy Providence is now begun. Give thy blessing to those who are chosen to teach and govern in this house. Let a deep sense of responsibility and of their obligations to thee fill their minds and hearts. Help them to train the hand, the mind and the heart to the love and the service of God, and to the love and the service of their fellow-men.

Almighty God, the source of all wisdom and holiness, who by thy Word and Spirit dost conduct all thy servants in the ways of peace and righteousness, inviting them by thy promises, winning them by long-suffering, and endearing them by thy loving-kindness; grant unto us so truly to repent of our sins, so carefully to reform our errors, so diligently to watch over all our actions, so industriously to perform all our duty, that we may never willingly transgress thy holy laws; but that it may be the work of our lives to obey thee, the joy of our souls to please thee, the satisfaction of all our hopes and the perfection of all our desires to live with thee, in the holiness of thy kingdom of grace and glory.

Almighty God, who hast given us grace at this time with one accord to make our common supplications unto thee; and dost promise that when two or three are gathered together in thy name, thou wilt grant their requests; fulfil

O Lord, the desires and petitions of thy servants, as may be most expedient for us ; granting us in this world knowledge of thy truth, and in the world to come life everlasting.

AMEN.

MR. HUEY then said :

Mr. Williamson was much concerned about the men whom he should intrust with the erection and maintenance of this school, and naturally turned to those in whom he had learned to confide. With the possible exception of his executor, Mr. Cummins, whom we have the pleasure of having with us this afternoon, there was no man with whom he consulted more freely and upon whose judgment he placed more dependence that Mr. Henry C. Townsend, who is now the Chairman of the Board of Trustees and who has been generous to a fault in his devotion of time and labor to the execution of Mr. Williamson's wishes in connection with the erection of these buildings. The Trustees were therefore unanimous in the belief that he of all others was the one best fitted and equipped to present to you this afternoon an account of what led up to the idea of this school, what has been done in connection with its curriculum and selection of students, and what the hopeful anticipations of the Trustees are for its future. I beg to introduce to you Mr. Henry C. Townsend.

ADDRESS BY HENRY C. TOWNSEND, CHAIRMAN OF THE
BOARD OF TRUSTEES.

In this locality, so near the spot on which William Penn
landed on his first visit to his province of Pennsylvania ; in
this presence composed largely of descendants of his followers in religious faith, and of citizens of Philadelphia, the city
of his creation, and on this occasion devoted to exercises
commemorative of the opening of a new Institution for free
instruction in useful and practical learning, it seems appro-
priate to give a short sketch of the history of public education in Pennsylvania, with a brief reference to the men who
may be regarded as its fathers and founders, and thus to show
a direct connection between them and The Williamson Free
School of Mechanical Trades.

Wickersham in his "History of Education in Pennsylvania,"
page 19 says :

"The root of much that is admirable in the history of
Pennsylvania, including her educational policy, can be traced
to certain doctrines of the Friends or Quakers, and to the
broad statesmanship of their leader in America, William
Penn."

The belief professed and doctrines taught by Friends, their
consistent lives and their silent, spiritual mode of worship,
were calculated to attract the thoughtful, the reflecting and
educated rather than the ignorant. Included in the membership of the society were such learned men and accomplished
scholars as George Fox, (who was originally a shoemaker,) of

whose Journal, Spurgeon, the distinguished Baptist preacher of London says:

"His life well repays the earnest student. It is a rich mine. Every page of it is as precious as solid gold. Books, nowadays, are hammered out, and you get but little metal in acres of leaves; but the Journal of George Fox contains ingots of gold, truths which require to be thought of month by month before you can get to the bottom of them." John Woolman, (who started in life as a tailor,) of whose Journal, Crabbe Robinson says in his diary, "A perfect gem. His is a beautiful Soul. An illiterate tailor, he writes in a style of the most exquisite purity and grace. His moral qualities are transferred to his writings. Had he not been so very humble, he would have written a still better book, for fearing to indulge in vanity, he conceals the events in which he was a great actor. His religion is love. His whole existence and all his passions were love;" and Charles Lamb says of him:

"Get the writings of John Woolman by heart and love the early Quakers."

Robert Barclay, Thomas Loe (by whose preaching William Penn was convinced of the truth as professed by Friends,) Thomas Ellwood, the pupil and friend of Milton, Edward Burroughs, Isaac Penfington, Arscott and Claridge.

"Among the early settlers of Pennsylvania might be named a long list of scholars and men of ability such as the accomplished James Logan, Penn's friend and secretary and the founder of the Loganian Library, Governors Thomas Lloyd and Andrew Hamilton, Pastorius, the Sage of Germantown, master of seven or eight languages, Kelpius, 'the learned mystic of the Wissahickon,' Keith and Makin, teachers and authors, David Lloyd, Christopher Taylor, a profound Latin, Greek and Hebrew scholar, Thomas Wynne, Story, Norris, Brooke and many others not less distinguished."

(Wickersham p. 26) and to which may be added such names as Samuel Carpenter, Edward Shippen, Anthony Morris, James Fox, William Markham, Israel Pemberton and others eminent in public affairs.

Judge Pennypacker in a recently published article entitled "The University of Pennsylvania in its relation to the State of Penna." (Penna. Mag. of History and Biography, No. 1, Vol. xv, p. 88,) says:

"The settlement of Pennsylvania being due to the unrest of the members of a religious sect whose advanced thought brought them into conflict with existing conditions in England, and the moral and mental breadth of its founder having led him to offer it as a home not only for those of his own way of thinking, but for all in that island and upon the continent who had in vain wrestled against intolerance, it was natural that his province should attract more men of learning than other colonies whose promoters were simply seeking for profit or were bent upon the enforcement of illiberal policies."

William Penn, the founder of the province which has developed into the great commonwealth of Pennsylvania, a wise and practical legislator, the most distinguished and successful colonizer of his time, was an accomplished student of Oxford University and a voluminous author. Of him an authority as eminent and impartial as the late Ch. Justice Sharswood said in an address before The Historical Society of Penna. :

"Our founder had well studied the science of government and laws, though he was no lawyer by profession. He drew his first principles on this subject from the most authoritative source. He held that 'the glory of God Almighty and the good of mankind are the reasons and the object of government and therefore government itself is a venerable ordinance of God.' "

Another of his principles subsequently adopted as the basis of the Declaration of Independence was that :

"Any government is free to the people under it whatever be its frame, where the laws rule and the people are a party to those laws, and more then this is tyranny, oligarchy and confusion.''

With this knowledge of the character of William Penn it is quite natural that we should find in his frame of government announced as early as April 25, 1682, a provision, ''that the Governor and Provincial Council shall erect and order all public schools and encourage and reward the authors of useful science and laudable inventions.''

He also in his ''Laws agreed upon in England'' following his '' Frame of the Government'' for his colony in sec. 28 provides

''That all children within this province of the age of twelve years, *shall be taught some useful trade or skill*, to the end none may be idle, but the poor may work to live, and *the rich, if they become poor, may not want.''* (*Charter to William Penn and Laws of Province of Pennsylvania passed* between 1682 and 1710 published by State of Pennsylvania 1879, p. 102.)

As early as the year 1683, before the worthy followers of Penn were comfortably housed on the margin of the Delaware, a pamphlet was published which is found in Thomas Budd's book entitled '' *Good order established in Pennsylvania and New Jersey*,'' published in 1685, from which the following extracts are made :

'' Now it might be well if a law were made by the Governors and General Assembly of Pennsylvania and New Jersey that all persons inhabiting in said provinces do put their children for seven years to the public school or longer if the parents please. Second.—That schools be provided in all towns and cities, and persons of known honesty, skill and understanding be yearly chosen by the Governor and General Assembly, to teach and instruct boys and girls, *in all the most useful arts and sciences*, that they, in their youth-

ful capacity may be capable to understand, (as the learning to read and write true English, Latin and other useful
speeches and languages, and fair writing, arithmetic and book-
keeping;) and the boys to be taught and instructed in some
mystery and trade, as making of mathematical instruments,
joinery, turnery, the making of clocks and watches, weav-
ing, shoe making, or any other trade or mystery the school
is capable of teaching; the girls to be taught and instructed
in spinning of flax and wool and knitting of gloves and
stockings, sewing and making of all sorts of needle work,
and the making of straw work, such as hats and baskets,
etc., or any other art or mystery that the school is capable of
teaching. Third.—That the scholars be kept in the morn-
ing two hours at reading, writing, book-keeping, etc., and
other two hours at that art, mystery or trade that he or
she most delighteth in, and then let them have two hours
to dine and for recreation; and in the afternoon two
hours in reading, writing etc., and the other two hours at
work at their several employments. Sixth.—Let 1000 acres
of land be given and laid out in a good place, to every public
school that shall be set up and the rent or income of it to go
towards the defraying of the charge of the school. Seventh.
—And to the end that the children of the poor people and
the children of Indians may have the like good learning
with the children of rich people, let them be maintained free
of charge to their parents out of the profits of the school
arising by the work of the scholars, by which the poor and
the Indians, as well as the rich, will have their children
taught; and the remainder of the profits, if any there be, to
be disposed of in the building of school houses and improvements on the 1000 acres of land which belong to the school.''

The suggestions and recommendations of this pamphlet
soon took practical effect, as at a meeting of a council of
Friends in Philadelphia, held 18th of Tenth month, (October) 1683, the following minute was adopted:

''The Governor (William Penn) and council having taken
into serious consideration the necessity there is for the instruction and sober education of youth in the town of Philadelphia, sent for Enoch Flower, an inhabitant of said town,
who, for twenty years past, hath been exercised in that
care and employment in England, to whom having com-

municated their minds, he embraced it upon the following terms :

To learn to read   English—4s. by the quarter.
 " " " " and write " 6s. " " "
 " " " "   "   " and
    cast accounts . . . 8s. " " "
For boarding a scholar, that is to say diet, washing, lodging and schooling 10£ for one whole year."

Six years later in 1689 the followers and contemporaries of William Penn imbued with his wise, practical and religious views, established and opened in Philadelphia "The Friends' Public School," which was incorporated by Deputy Governor Markham in 1697, and later confirmed by fresh patent from William Penn, the final one bearing date Eleventh month (November) 29th, 1711, the objects of the corporation being stated in the following preamble :

"Whereas the prosperity and welfare of any people depend in great measure upon the good education of youth and their early introduction into the principles of true religion and virtue, and qualifying them to serve their country and themselves, by breeding them in reading, writing, and learning of languages and *useful arts and science*, suitable to their age, sex, and degree which cannot be effected in any manner so well, as by erecting public schools for the purposes aforesaid."

This is the foundation and origin of The Penn Charter School now located on Twelfth Street near Market, Philadelphia, which has been in successful operation from that time to the present.

"George Keith, formerly of Aberdeen, Scotland, was the first teacher of this School, who at the end of a year was followed by Thomas Makin, who is described as having been a good "Latinist." Several schools have been maintained and are still in operation under the provisions of this original charter." *History of West Town Boarding School, Ed. of 1884, p. 12.*

The precepts, teaching and work of William Penn and his followers and contemporaries in the direction of public education thus had their effect during the provincial and colonial period of our State's History, forming a healthy public sentiment on that subject, which was in full operation when in the year 1723 Benjamin Franklin, at the age of seventeen became a resident of Philadelphia. His practical character, his strong common sense and natural strength of mind found in that community a congenial home, a people with whom he could work with hearty good-will and by whom, the force of his character and abilities in all useful directions, was soon felt and fully recognized. If asked to name the men who above and beyond all others, by the weight of their character, the wisdom of their counsel and the excellence of their work, accomplished the most successful results in the cause of public education in Pennsylvania, the community of the present day, guided in the expression of its opinion by the weight of historical authority, would with entire unanimity say, William Penn in the provincial or colonial period, and Benjamin Franklin in the revolutionary period of the State's History.

The effect of these sentiments and the influence of these early colonists of Pennsylvania on the subject of public education are seen in the provision made in the original and temporary Constitution framed for the State of Pennsylvania in the year 1776, soon after the Declaration of Independence was proclaimed, in the following language :

" A school or schools shall be established in each county for the convenient instruction of youth with such salaries to the masters *paid by the public*, as may enable them to instruct youth at low prices ; and all useful learning shall be duly encouraged and promoted in one or more Universities.''

And by Act of Assembly of April 7th, 1786, passed soon after the successful close of the Revolutionary war, it was enacted :

''That sixty thousand acres of land, part of the unappropriated lands belonging to the State, be and they are hereby reserved and appropriated for the sole and express purpose of *endowing public schools* in the different counties of this State agreeably to the said fourty-fourth section of the Constitution.''

The constitutional convention of 1789-90 also made the following provision :

''The legislature shall, as soon as conveniently may be, provide by law for the establishment of schools throughout the State, in such manner *that the poor may be taught gratis.*''

This article was also incorporated into the Constitution of 1838 and continued to be the only constitutional provision on the subject of education until 1874.

As early as 1794 a legislative committee made a report on this subject outlining a plan which was a near approach to the subsequent free school system of the state. The successive Governors of Pennsylvania, McKean, Snyder, Findlay, Heister and Shulze all urged the importance of free public education upon the legislatures, which resulted in some legislation upon that subject in 1803, 1804, 1809 and 1818, which went so far only as to provide for the payment of the education of the children of the poor in the then existing, ordinary private schools. As early as 1810, Nicholas

Biddle, a man of rare intellectual powers and a member of the Legislature at the early age of twenty-four, whose chief historical distinction arose from his presidency of the United States Bank for eighteen years, who was, however, as great in statesmanship and scholarship as he was in finance, introduced and advocated a bill for general free education which was the basis of the subsequent legislation of 1834. It was not, however, until the latter year, viz., 1834, that under the active efforts of such friends of education as Governor Wolf, Senators Joseph B. Anthony and N. B. Fetterman, and also Nicholas Biddle, Robert Vaux, Joseph R. Chandler, Dr. George Smith, Thaddeus Stevens, Benjamin Mathias, Joseph G. Clarkson, William Martin, Samuel Breck, Charles B. Penrose, James Thompson, John Wiegand, Thomas H. Burroughs, Dr. Wilmer Worthington and other eminent Pennsylvanians, many of them members of the Legislature, the law entitled "An Act to establish a general system of education by common school" was passed.

It is interesting to note that the legislative committee, charged with the duty of inquiring into and reporting on that subject, also give attention to manual labor education by reporting in favor of that system, saying among other things.

"First.—That the expense of education, when connected with manual labor judiciously directed, may be reduced at least one-half.

Second.—That the exercise of about three hours manual labor daily, contributes to the health and cheerfulness of the pupil, by strengthening and improving his physical powers, and by engaging his mind in useful pursuits.

Third.—That so far from manual labor being an impediment to the progress of the pupil in intellectual studies, it has been found in proportion as one pupil excelled another in the amount of labor performed, the same pupil has excelled the other, in equal ratio, in his intellectual studies.

Fourth.—That manual labor institutions tend to break down the distinctions between rich and poor which exist in society, inasmuch as they give an almost equal opportunity of education to the poor by labor, as is afforded to the rich by the possession of wealth.

Fifth.—That pupils trained in this way are much better fitted for active life, and better qualified to act as useful citizens, than when educated in any other mode,—that they are better as regards physical energy, and better intellectually and morally.''

From the above citations it will be seen that schools for the mental (as distinguished from the mechanical) education of the youth of both sexes, as well in the ordinary as in the advanced branches of learning, have existed and flourished in this State since the days of the early colonists, contributing largely to the formation of the character of its people and the development of its natural resources. It is however, only recently that the *industrial* education of the youth of our land has become a subject of serious thought and practical application. It has been forced upon the attention of observing and reflecting persons, who have realized that several causes have contributed to the decadence of the American apprenticeship system, prominent among which may be mentioned, First—the enormous expansion during the past thirty years of every kind of mechanical enterprise and the consequent enrichment of the proprietors :—the master ceased to be the shop companion of the apprentice, and no longer taught him by his example, or imparted to him the traditions and rules of his art. The master found his services to be of much greater value in the office than in the shop and the relation of apprenticeship was neglected.

Secondly—the automatic power tool was introduced to replace many of the slow, hand processes which gave employment to the skilled mechanic. It was believed by many that this machinery would supplant him altogether and that inferior labor only was needed for the workshop, also by others that skilled mechanics were only required as foremen and fitters up of the finished output of the shop.

Many manufacturers have found it more profitable to teach men certain parts of the trade, knowing that by this method the operator would more certainly remain in his employ, as he would not be sufficiently learned in the trade to obtain work elsewhere, unless at an establishment engaged in the same line of work. It was also ascertained that skilled mechanics soon became tired of one kind of labor and if compelled to continue at it, would seek other employment less monotonous.

One of the earliest steps in this country in the direction of manual training was taken at the Naval Academy at Annapolis in 1868, and the instruction of the officers of our Navy in the use of mechanic's tools has steadily grown in importance to the present time.

The Russian Manual school exhibit at the Centennial Exhibition did much towards popularizing thought on the subject, and public attention and interest in it have been growing steadily ever since.

The St. Louis University, the Boston Institute of Technology and Cornell University were the first institutions to add mechanical laboratories to their equipments, and thus prepare for this new and important feature in education.

The Worcester Institute, Worcester, Mass., was soon after started, and the Spring Garden Institute, Philadelphia, was the fourth manual training school of size to be inaugurated in the country.

Girard College and the Chicago Manual Training School, followed soon afterwards.

In 1885 Philadelphia added the Manual Training School to its public schools, and enjoys the distinction of being the first city in the world to make that branch a part of the system of free public education.

In the same year the University of Michigan at Ann Arbor added mechanical shops and training to its equipment and curriculum, and now ranks high as a manual training school.

The Pratt Institute of Brooklyn, N. Y. founded in 1886 has well furnished departments for various mechanical trades.

San Francisco has perhaps the finest and best equipped manual training schools in the world, and the University of Pennsylvania has a complete manual training department for her mechanical engineering students, started in 1889.

By the generosity of Dr. Zenas Barnum of Baltimore, Md., in his bequest of $80,000 for that purpose, there has been recently added to The McDonough School near that city a department for instruction and practice in manual training, limited at present to wood working.

The Toledo Manual Training School of Toledo, Ohio, is also a well equipped institution with eleven shops or laboratories, and three hundred and eighty pupils who do their Academic work in the Public High School to which the Manual Training School is attached as an annex.

The Drexel Institute now almost completed, will be one of the leading Institutes of the World for the training of the hand in harmony with the development of the intellectual faculties.

Fortunate indeed is our country in the establishment of manual training in every section of its broad dominion, and no city is more favored in this respect than our own Philadelphia.

A step further and we reach the Trade Schools.

In Albemarle Co., Virginia, there is the Miller Manual Labor School endowed by the will of Samuel Miller, which started with an invested fund of over one million of dollars, and under the able charge of Captain Vawter is doing a wonderfully good work for that section of our land, limited in its admission of pupils, however, to the residents of that county.

The New York Trade School founded, developed and maintained by the intelligent and comprehensive thought and generosity of Col. Richard T. Auchmuty, is conferring vast benefits on its scholars, who come from all parts of our Union, and thus spread the effects of its good works all over the Continent.

The Master Builder's Trade School of Philadelphia established on a broad basis and wisely conducted, has entered upon a career of wide usefulness.

And now we have this The Williamson Free School of Mechanical Trades, different in some respects from any other trade school previously established, and designed, as far as a school can be, to take the place of the old fashioned apprenticeship when the master and the learner were in close contact, but based we think on broader, more intelligent and more comprehensive ideas as to the proper manner of teaching boys the art and mystery of various mechanical trades and in the hope of reaching more practical results.

The New York Trade School of Col. Auchmuty, the Master Builders' Trade School of Phila. and The Williamson Free School of Mechanical Trades are all steps in advance of the Manual Training Schools inasmuch as they teach the boy his trade complete in addition to the sleight of hand taught at the other institutions.

Many persons thought it impracticable to teach a trade complete at a school until Colonel Auchmuty proved that it could be done.

The germ of the idea which has taken visible expression in The Williamson Free School of Mechanical Trades may be found in the memorable letter of William Penn, addressed to his wife and children on the eve of his departure from England in 1682, to make his first visit to his colony. A letter so valuable for its wisdom, so touching in its pathos, so beautiful in its simplicity, so full of tender affection and solicitude for the temporal and spiritual welfare of those near and dear to him, to make it worthy of an honored place in the library of this or any other school. In regard to the education of his children he says :

"For their learning be liberal. Spare no cost; for by such parsimony all that is saved is lost, but let it be *useful knowledge*, (such as is consistent with truth and godliness, not cherishing a vain conversation or idle mind) but ingenuity *mixed with industry* is good for the body and mind too. I recommend the useful parts of mathematics and building houses or ships, measuring, surveying, dialing, navigation, but agriculture is especially in my eye. Let my children be husbandmen and housewives; industrious, healthy, honest and of good example, (like Abraham and the holy ancients, who pleased God and obtained a good report.) This leads to consider the works of God and nature, things that are good, and diverts the mind from being taken up with the vain arts and inventions of a luxurious world. It is commendable in the Princes of Germany and the Nobles of that Empire that they have all their children *instructed by some useful occupation*" (intimating that in certain contingences a trade was a better thing as a steady reliance than a throne.) "Be sure to observe their genius and do not cross it as to learning; let them not dwell too long on one thing, but let their change be agreeable and all their diversions have some little bodily labor in them."

And in a communication of a later date quoted by Proud in his History of Pennsylvania, Wm. Penn says :

"Upon the whole matter I undertake to say that if we would preserve our government we must endear it to the people. To do this, beside the necessity of presenting just and wise views *we must secure the youth* ; this is not to be done but by the amendment of the way of education, and that with all eminent speed and diligence. I say the government is highly obliged : it is a sort of *Trustee for the youth* of the kingdom, who though minors yet, will have the government when we are gone. Therefore depress vice and cherish virtue, that through good education they may become good which will truly render them happiness in this world and a great way fitted for that which is to come. If this is done they will owe more to your memories for their education than for their estates.''

As an illustration of the saying that good may sometimes be evolved from evil it is due to truth to say that The Williamson Free School of Mechanical Trades, the opening of which we here and now celebrate, is the direct outcome and result of the discontinuance of the apprenticeship system of labor in many trades. It was the knowledge of this fact, operating upon the practical common sense and the benevolent heart of I. V. Williamson, that induced him to devote so large a portion of his well-earned fortune to the erection and endowment of this School for the intelligent and practical education of the youth of our land in useful trades.

In many conversations with the speaker on this occasion, while formulating his plans and discussing the provisions of his contemplated deed of trust, he was very emphatic in his recognition of this condition as one of the evils of modern society, and equally so in the expression of his sense of duty to do what was in his power to correct this injustice to the youth of our land. In his Endowment Deed of Trust, dated December First, A.D. 1888, he states his motives and intentions, and among others makes the following recitals.

''WHEREAS, The subject of the proper training and education of youth to habits of industry and economy, and the importance of their learning trades, so that they may be able to earn their living by the labor of their hands, has for a long time received my careful attention ;

AND WHEREAS, I am convinced that the abandonment or disuse of the good old custom of apprenticeship to trades has resulted in many young men growing up in idleness, which leads to vice and crime and is fraught with great danger to society ;

AND WHEREAS, I am impressed with the belief that in many worthy institutions founded for the free education of the young, and sometimes even in the public schools, the system and course of education, and the associations and surroundings connected therewith, often unfit a young man for a life of manual labor, and induce a false belief in his mind that to labor with his hands is not respectable—and for this reason professional and mercantile pursuits are over-crowded with incompetent candidates who meet with failure —and thus many who, if they had been differently trained in early life, could have supported themselves at some trade in comfort and decency, are condemned to idleness and often to dissipation, beggary and crime ;

AND WHEREAS, For nearly thirty years I have carefully considered this subject, with the intention at the proper time of founding and endowing a free institution, to be located in the City of Philadelphia or its vicinity, where, subject to the control of proper managers and under the direction and supervision of skillful and expert instructors, poor and deserving boys could be gratuitously instructed in the rudiments of a good English education and what is of equal, if not greater, importance, trained to habits of industry and economy and taught such mechanical trades or handicrafts as may be suited to their several capacities, so that when they arrive at manhood they may be able to support themselves decently by the labor of their own hands and become useful and respectable members of society ; as I am well convinced that in this country any able-bodied young man of industrious and economical habits who has learned a good mechanical trade can not only earn a good living and acquire an independence, but also become a useful and respected citizen ;

AND WHEREAS, The time has now arrived at which I can put my long-cherished intention into effect, and devote and dedicate to the object a sufficent fund out of means which have been saved and accumulated for the purpose ;

NOW, KNOW ALL MEN BY THESE PRESENTS, That I, Isaiah V. Williamson, of the City of Philadelphia, merchant, in order to carry out the object I so long have had in view, in the hope of supplying a long-felt want in the community, and with the intention and design of founding and endowing

in perpetuity an institution to be known as "The Williamson Free School of Mechanical Trades," and hereinafter
designated as the School, do hereby make, constitute, and
appoint my friends John Baird, James C. Brooks, Lemuel
Coffin, Edward Longstreth, William C. Ludwig, Henry C.
Townsend and John Wanamaker, all of the City of Philadelphia, and their successors in the trust appointed or
created as hereinafter directed, the Trustees to hold the title
to, erect, equip, maintain, direct and manage the school
upon, under, and subject to the trusts, confidences, and
conditions hereinafter declared of and concerning the same,
which said Trustees, and their successors in the trust, shall
be known as the Trustees of the Williamson Free School of
Mechanical Trades, and are in this deed hereafter designated
the Trustees, and whose names I have hereinabove inserted
in alphabetical order so as to remove any impression of
preference on my part for either or any, which might otherwise be drawn from the order in which they have been named.

"I leave to the judgment and discretion of the Trustees
the character, number and extent of the said buildings to be
erected, but as the great object to be attained is to board,
lodge, clothe, and instruct in mechanical trades those who,
when arrived at manhood, will be obliged to labor with their
hands for their support, I particularly direct that all palatial
structures, expensive materials, and elaborate ornamentation
or decorations shall be avoided, so that the scholars may not
by reason of luxurious or expensive accommodations and
surroundings acquire tastes or habits which may unfit them
for their trades in the sphere of life in which their lots are
to be cast."

While leaving to the discretion of the Trustees the whole
subject of the studies to be taught, he says :

"I request that they shall at all times bear in mind the
fact that the main object I have in view is to train young
men to mechanical trades, so that they may earn their own
living, and that while the acquisition of any branch of an
English education which may be of aid to them in their
several trades is necessary and important, any higher or
advanced knowledge, which might render them dissatisfied
with or unfit for their employments, is unnecessary and may
be disadvantageous. I expressly direct that each and every
scholar shall be compelled to learn and be thoroughly in-

structed in one good mechanical trade, so that when they leave the school on the completion of their indentures they may be able to support themselves by the labor of their own hands. I leave to the discretion of the Trustees the selection of the several kinds of mechanical trades to be taught, and the determination of the particular one that shall be taught to and acquired by each scholar but I particularly desire that the taste, capacity, intelligence, and adaptability of each scholar be ascertained and considered before assigning him to any particular trade."

"I desire and direct that the moral and religious training of the scholars shall be properly looked after and cared for by the Trustees, but that there shall be no attempt by the Trustees at proselytism among the scholars, and no favoritism shown by the Trustees to any particular sect or creed. I especially direct that each scholar shall be taught to speak the truth at all times, and I particularly direct and charge as an imperative duty upon the Trustees that each and every scholar shall be thoroughly trained to habits of frugality, economy and industry, as above all others the one great lesson which I desire to have impressed upon every scholar and inmate of the School, is that in this country every able-bodied, healthy young man who has learned a good mechanical trade, and is truthful, honest, frugal, temperate, and industrious, is certain to succeed in life, and to become a useful and respected member of society."

"I desire and direct that the physical training of the scholars shall be carefully attended to, that they shall have proper exercise and recreation, so that so far as such a result can be brought about by training and care, each one may grow up with a sound mind in a strong body."

The par value of the securities transferred by the deed, composed entirely of stocks of various corporations, was $1,596,000 having an appraised value at the then market price, of $2,119,25 and producing at that time an income approximating $100,000.

In view of the recent decision of the Court of Appeals of the State of New York, declaring void and inoperative, the will of Hon. Samuel J. Tilden, by which he attempted to give several millions of dollars for the erection and endowment of a free public library, the wisdom of Mr. Williamson in founding his Free School of Mechanical Trades in his life time and thus avoiding the perils of hostile litigation, cannot be too highly recommended as an example worthy of imitation by all contemplating similar objects.

Soon after the delivery of this deed Mr. Williamson addressed to each of the Trustees a letter so characteristic of the man, so indicative of the active interest he felt in this work that it is here given at full length :

PHILADELPHIA, December 13th, 1888.

To MESSRS. JOHN BAIRD, JAMES C. BROOKS, LEMUEL COFFIN, EDWARD LONGSTRETH, WILLIAM C. LUDWIG, HENRY C. TOWNSEND AND JOHN WANAMAKER, TRUSTEES.

GENTLEMEN :—I send you herewith a number of applications for the sale of lands, and several pamphlets and other documents, relating to industrial schools and institutions, which have from time to time been sent to me, and all of which I now refer to you.

I have also thought it proper and fitting that, at the beginning of the undertaking, I should bring to your attention my own views about the details of the establishment and the management of the School, and submit for your consideration, some suggestions of my own, which have been the result of patient and careful consideration of the subject which is now committed to your hands. The first point of importance is the selection and purchase of the land. My own judgment is in favor of some site on the upper Neshaminy, in the vicinity of Langhorne or Newtown, as I am impressed with the healthfulness of the location, and I have some natural inclination in favor of my native County of Bucks. Some farm property on the Neshaminy, near the crossing of the Bound Brook Branch of the North Pennsylvania Railroad, has been offered to me by a Mr. Wildman, with whom I am now in correspondence, and some other lands near Newtown have recently been brought to my attention by Mr. John M. Stapler. I should be glad if you would visit both properties with me, in order to see whether in your opinion, either of them is suitable for the purpose, and can be purchased at a reasonable price.

Until the question of the purchase of land is decided, it seems to me that it would be well to defer taking any action upon plans or buildings. Otherwise, you may be run down and wearied by applications from architects and contractors before you have had time to consider the question of the character and extent of the buildings that may be required.

Upon this subject of buildings and the resulting one of the proper method of lodging, boarding and managing boys, I am decidedly in favor of what is called "Home Life," as distinguished from that of one large Institution ; and, from all I have read and reflected upon the subject, I think the advantages of the former system are as follows :—

1. The boys will be under better moral control by being inmates of small homes and having the advantages of home life.

2. It avoids the necessity of large structures, and the consequent temptation to erect imposing buildings and make an architectural display.

3. It enables you to feel your way, and to provide from time to time, only such buildings as can readily be filled by scholars ; whereas, if the other plan of one large institute is adopted, there might be a much larger expenditure made than would actually be required for those who apply for admission.

If you agree with me in these views, I would suggest that upon purchasing a site, the farm buildings upon the place, if there are any, should at once be utilized by taking in as many boys as they will accommodate, and such boys could at once be assigned to learn the trade of mason, carpenter, bricklayer, or other similar occupation, and be occupied in the erecting of new buildings and the preparation and cultivation of the ground. If there should be a quarry on the land, and a deposit of good clay, contracts could at once be made for quarrying building stone by the perch, and making bricks per thousand ; and, with the materials thus ready to hand, additional small houses could from time to time be built and occupied, when completed, with new boys. Each house when completed could be placed under the charge of some experienced mechanic to be employed as an instructor, and with whose family the boys could be boarders, and thus the daily and domestic lives of the boys would be under the influence of a frugal and industrious mechanic's home, and be somewhat similar to that which formerly existed when, apprentices to trades were inmates of their master's family.

It would, of course, be necessary at some time to erect some central and convenient building for common school purposes for the younger scholars, and also probably some large room or hall for religious and other instructions by lectures, etc., but my own judgment is that such a building should not be commenced until it is demonstrated that the school will be a success, and until the number of inmates is sufficient to justify the expenditure. In the meantime, it may probably be found that some farm house or other farm buildings, with slight alterations and repairs, would answer the purpose for some years, during which the unexpended Building Fund would be increasing at compound interest, and, in a few years, furnish out of its accretions a new fund sufficient for the central buildings.

I am inclined to think that it would be better to locate the School near to some thriving or growing country town or village, containing churches of different denominations, which the boys could attend. Thus each boy could worship at the church and receive religious instruction from the denomination in which he had been brought up, and the occasional mingling with the outer world will be of service to the boys.

I have prepared this letter with no intention of controlling your own judgments upon the various matters touched upon ; but, as I have devoted a great deal of time to the consideration of the questions, and feel a deep interest in the success of the undertaking, I have thought it best to give you my own views upon these matters, which, by the Foundation Deed, I have left entirely to your own discretion..

Very respectfully,

[SIGNED] I. V. WILLIAMSON.

Soon after its appointment the Board organized by the election of John Baird as Chairman, James C. Brooks as Treasurer, and Alfred Helmbold as Secretary, and on January 4th, 1889, John M. Shrigley as Assistant Secretary, and June 1st, 1889, as General Manager and Secretary, followed at a later date November 2d, 1889, by the election of Robert Crawford as Superintendent, and on June 6th, 1890, John M. Shrigley was elected President of the School.

In the selection of these two gentlemen for the important executive positions which represent the actual working of the School, the Trustees have realized that they have been most fortunate. Both are especially well qualified by temperament, experience and knowledge for their respective positions, and both have displayed the greatest possible zeal, fidelity, and ability in their work.

One of the first and most important duties imposed upon the Trustees was the selection of a proper site for the buildings. Guided by the limitations of the Foundation Deed as to area, locality and cost they visited several farms to which their attention was called by persons desirous of selling and always accompanied by I. V. Williamson, who as long as he lived attended their meetings and manifested a lively interest not only in the selection of a site but in all other plans and projects that claimed attention, and finally after a careful consideration of all the features attending the different sites visited, they concluded that the land on the line of the West Chester and Philadelphia Railroad, in Middletown Township, Delaware County, between Elwyn and Glen Riddle stations, about sixteen miles from Philadelphia, was in all respects the most suitable for the purposes in view.

After a brief negotiation they secured the title to four tracts of land embracing an area of about 200 acres, the lowest part adjoining the railroad having an elevation of 220 feet, and the summit selected as the site for the buildings, having an elevation of 310 feet above tide water of the Delaware, commanding an extensive view of the surrounding country, absolutely free from malaria or other unhealthy influences and having within its borders an abundant supply of pure spring water, and good building stone. The selection of this site was approved by I. V. Williamson, who was able to visit it but a few days before his last illness, and expressed in warm terms not only his satisfaction, but pleasure in the choice ; and this approval was the last business act of his life.

On the seventeenth day of May, 1889, the purchase was completed by the conveyance of the land to the Trustees for the consideration of $46,489.80.

The next important subject claiming their attention was the consideration and adoption of plans for the buildings. For these, proposals were invited from five of the leading architects of Philadelphia with equal compensation to all for their work whether accepted or not, and after a thorough examination of all that were offered, those submitted by Furness, Evans & Co. were adopted.

Ground was broken on the first day of May, 1890, the corner stone was laid on the eighth day of November, 1890, and under the direction of the competent and experienced architects, assisted by the almost daily watchful and skilled superintendence of President Shrigley and Superintendent Crawford, whose services in this respect have been invaluable, the work of erecting the buildings consisting of the large Administration building with a capacity (in its executive department such as recitation rooms, auditorium, dining hall, &c., for three hundred boys, seventy of whom are now here), the boiler and laundry house, work shop No. 1 and Superintendent's residence proceeded with all the rapidity consistent with good workmanship and safe results, until their final finish ready for occupancy on the twentieth day of October, inst. and you are now here to examine and we trust to approve of their adaptation to the uses for which they are designed.

The expenditure for lands, buildings, improvements of all kinds and furniture up to this time has been $237,600, while the income from both the endowment and building funds has been $295,500.

The rooms in the main building now occupied as dormitories will, when the cottages are finished, be used for draughting, library and museum purposes.

Of the seven trustees named by I. V. Williamson in his foundation deed, one of their number, William C. Ludwig, died on September 2d, 1889, honored, beloved and respected by all who knew him, and Col. Charles H. Banes, was on October 5th, 1889, elected to fill the vacancy.

Another original Trustee, John Baird, resigned on February 28th, 1890, and John H. Catherwood, on May 10th, 1890, was elected to fill the vacancy, and Col. Charles H. Banes resigned on September 11th, 1890, and Samuel B. Huey was on December 12th, 1890, elected to fill that vacancy.

They have after careful consideration, and in conformity with Mr. Williamson's wishes in that respect deemed it best to adopt in the management of the School, as near as is possible, the home rather than the institutional life for its scholars. Their plan contemplates separate and distinct cottages, each with a capacity for twenty-four boys, with heads for each family in the nature of father and mother. With this idea in view they have commenced three cottages near the Main Building which they expect to have finished by April 1st next, when forty-eight more boys can be admitted, and they propose to continue the erection of additional cottages as rapidly as their means will permit.

The Trustees desire to say thus publicly while fully realizing the magnitude and importance of their work and anxious to discharge it to the best of their ability and desirous of avoiding all mistakes, they have from the start felt somewhat embarrassed by the fact, that they were obliged to act without the benefit of the experience of any similar school. So far as they have been able to discover, there nowhere exists a mechanical trade school working in the exact lines prescribed in the Foundation Deed of Mr. Williamson, which must necessarily control their action. While he is liberal in giving them a very wide discretion, his views and wishes in many respects outside of the provisions of the deed, have been expressed verbally to them and they feel obliged to conform to them so far as is possible. They have naturally felt that much of their work must be tentative and experimental, that they must act upon that knowledge which comes only from actual experience. They have so far worked and will continue to do. so with the single purpose of achieving practical results. In the language of Abraham Lincoln, in his memorable letter to Horace Greely written in reply to some impatient public criticisms by the latter as to his dilatory action in the conduct of the war, "We will try to correct errors when shown to be errors and will adapt new views as soon as they shall appear to be true views." Hence they have not deemed it wise to prescribe in advance the actual trades among the many mentioned in the deed which shall be taught to the exclusion of others. Much in this direction must be left to the future, to the results of experience and to the natural tastes of the pupils, assisted by the judgment of the President, Superintendent and instructors.

They have, however, after much careful consideration of that subject, determined that the lowest limit as to age of admission shall be fifteen years, as they believe that a better mechanic can be turned out after three years' education begun at that or a later age, than after a longer apprenticeship begun at an earlier age, when a boy is too young to understand his duties, opportunities and responsibilities, and they will also be thereby enabled from the limited income to give a larger number of boys the advantages of the School.

They believe that the educated mechanic must necessarily be a more efficient force in the world's workshop than the ignorant—that the training of the mind, the eye and the hand should go on together—that manual training directed by intelligence produces a greater result at less cost—and that every tool wielded by a hand which is guided and controlled by a cultivated mind, must necessarily work more efficiently and would seem almost to acquire in its movement and action some of that intelligence by which it is directed.

They can only add that their earnest efforts will, in the future as they have been in the past, be directed to securing in the best manner and by the most approved methods, the object so near the heart of the benevolent founder of this Institute, viz. : the intelligent education of boys into skilled practical mechanics who, when they leave this school with its certificate of proficiency, will be able in his own words, "not only to earn a good living and acquire an independence, but also become useful and respected citizens."

Of Isaiah Vansant Williamson, the speaker on this occasion who knew him for forty years, felt it a duty a few years before his decease, in order to correct some public misrepresentations made in a daily paper, to publish the following communication :

JUSTICE TO A GOOD CITIZEN.

EDITOR OF THE EVENING BULLETIN. SIR:—The taste which prompts the enterprising newspaper writer to spread before the public the habits of daily life, the peculiarities of disposition, the personal appearance and the pecuniary affairs of the private citizen is very questionable, even when the state.

ments are correct, but when, from ignorance or a desire to amuse, misrepresentations are made, the practice is reprehensible. The article from the pen of "Bystander," in the *Daily News* of October 3d, relating to the venerable I. V. Williamson, while correct in many respects and well meant, contains some errors and is not in tone respectful towards one of Philadelphia's most generous and at the same time modest citizens. A just and accurate sketch of the character of such a man as Mr. Williamson, who is a conspicuous example of great business success combined with personal worth and becoming modesty, might be of value in stimulating others to imitate his example in the judicious use of wealth, acquired by industry, intelligence, integrity and self-denial. Any one desiring accuracy could have ascertained the truth in relation to Mr. Williamson from any of his numerous friends associated with him in many important business enterprises. They know him as a warm-hearted and genial friend, a liberal and judicious dispenser of his means, modest, quiet and unassuming in manner, and extremely averse to any public mention of his name in connection with his charities. His habits of domestic life and methods of distributing his bounty, while not peculiar, are exclusively his own affair and not properly the subject of public notice. While his benefactions have been liberal in amount, they are characterized by good judgment and a broad and comprehensive spirit of sympathy with educational progress and the relief of suffering humanity in all its forms, free from all sectarian bias. He does not lead the narrow and meagre life implied in the article referred to, nor does he have " his habitation over a store in Bank Street," but lives modestly as a gentleman of his tastes and means should live, in a comfortable home in a central part of the city, where he is accessible to his few, but congenial, personal friends. Nor is it true as stated that he has no one to help him in his business affairs. Fortunately he is still vigorous in mind and body, and continues to exercise his habits of industry and method in the management of his business ; but he does employ a capable and competent assistant in some of its details. One who knows his modest and retiring disposition, his quiet and simple tastes, his liberal and judicious contributions, made in the most unobstrusive manner, to many deserving charities, feels that the correction of some of the errors in the article referred to, calculated to give a wrong impression of a worthy man, is only a simple act of Justice.

(The above well-deserved tribute to a good citizen is sent without the knowledge of the respected gentleman to whom it refers, and is only published to correct a few probably inadvertent errors in a recent interesting sketch of Mr. Williamson in another paper.)—[EDITOR BULLETIN.]

On a recent occasion complimentary to Dr. Edward Brooks upon his assuming the responsible position of Superintendent of public education in Philadelphia, Judge Fell gave expression to the following truthful sentiment :

" Many of the aims and ambitions of life are mere delusions—much for which we labor and struggle is not worth the effort.

The truest estimate of the success of a human life is the
measure of its benefit to others.

No man's life has been successful if it has not been of
honest usefulness and worth to his fellow-men.''

Applying this test to the record of the life of I. V.
Williamson, we must all admit it was a success.

He was born in Falsington, Bucks County, Pennsylvania,
February 3d, 1803. His parents were Mahlon Williamson
and Charity Vansant, both descendants of a long line of
ancestors connected with the religious society of Friends,
and if it be true, as is believed by many, that the foundation
of character in after life rests upon and grows out of the
home life and surroundings of the young, it may be safely
asserted that the principles taught and the examples furnished by those worthy parents, contributed largely to the
formation of that character which he established in early
manhood and maintained to the end—a character made up
largely of self-denial, self-reliance, honesty, truthfulness, integrity and industry.

His earliest ancestor on the paternal side to emigrate to
this country, and from whom he was the fifth in the line
of descent, was Duncan Williamson, a Scotchman, who
came here in or about the year 1661, some twenty years before the landing of William Penn, as we find him recorded
as a Juryman at the Upland Court (at Chester) in 1678, (the
first Jury known to have been drawn in this county,) and he
took up under patent from the Duke of York (from whom
William Penn subsequently obtained his grant of the province,) one tract of about 100 acres of land on the east bank

of the Schuylkill river near its mouth and another tract of 100 acres (increased by subsequent purchases) on the South side of the Neshaminy in Bensalem Township, Bucks County, and extending to the Delaware river, about four miles south of the present city of Bristol, on which he established the ferry across the Delaware river to the site of the present city of Beverly, New Jersey, known down to a recent period as "Dunk's Ferry" named after him, as he was generally known as "Dunk" Williamson.

In early life I. V. Williamson attended the local school of the district, which was only open during the winter months, and his school education was of course restricted to the limited opportunities then furnished. The quiet life on his father's farm soon became irksome and his inclinations early turned to mercantile pursuits, and at thirteen years of age he was behind the counter of Harvey Gillingham's store at Falsington, where he remained as a clerk until his majority, obtaining there that knowledge of business methods, the use of which was the foundation of his subsequent fortune. He formed at that early period of his life and practiced rigidly those habits of strict economy as to personal expenditure and the careful investment and re-investment of any surplus means, which continued throughout his long life.

When he completed his apprenticeship, he went to Philadelphia in the year 1825, and opened a retail dry goods store on Second near Pine Street, where he remained but a few months and then formed a partnership with William Burton and moved his place of business to Second Street and

Coombe's Alley, and at the end of one year this partnership was dissolved and he bought the store of John S. Newlin, No. 9 North Second Street, succeeding him in business and carrying it on alone assisted by H. Nelson Burroughs as a clerk, who still survives an honored representative of that class of Philadelphia merchants who established its well earned and still maintained reputation for enterprise, integrity and fair dealing. Rigid economy practically applied was the order of the day in that period, and it was the habit of Mr. Williamson and his assistant in order to save cartage, to carry or with the aid of a wheel-barrow, to transport the goods bought at auction to the store.

Mr. Williamson formed a partnership with Mr. Burroughs in 1834 which continued until January 1st, 1837, when he finally retired from active business as a merchant, and the firm of Williamson, Burroughs & Clark was formed of which Mahlon Williamson, a younger brother was an active member, and I. V. Williamson was the special partner.

The fortune which he had then accumulated amounted to about $200,000 and he had the reputation of being the richest young merchant in Philadelphia who had made his money by his own exertions. Soon after this time he visited Europe travelling at will through its various parts, including Russia, and remaining abroad about one year. Upon his return, he refused to live the life of the idler, and engaged actively in a variety of public enterprises, investing his means wisely and liberally in various directions of general usefulness and in the development of the natural resources of his State and Country.

His nature in financial operations was cautious and conservative—he was an operator and investor rather than a speculator. He seldom or never bought with the sole object of making a sale with a profit, and in his operations he exercised a wise sagacity and careful prudence ; he would purchase stocks or bonds or real estate, at prices which his judgment, formed after careful consideration, led him to believe were low, and hold on to them until time and circumstances had increased their value. When he reached the age of about seventy, his fortune probably amounted to about $4,000,000 and at that period of his life, yielding to the impulses of his naturally kindly and sympathetic nature, keenly alive and responsive to the claims of all forms of suffering humanity, and regarding himself as only a steward of the large fortune which he had acquired by a life of integrity, self-denial, industry and intelligent efforts, he began a system of wise, judicious and liberal distribution of his means, giving in various directions and for a variety of purposes, in a broad and catholic spirit, both money and property, to hospitals, schools, homes and similar charitable and educational organizations. The aggregate of his donations during this period of his life from the age of seventy to eighty-six, while not known during his life time, was ascertained after his decease to have amounted to (including the endowment of this School) about $5,000,000, a sum believed to be larger than that ever given by any one individual in his life time in this country for benevolent purposes,—and after these liberal gifts, his estate amounted at the time of his decease to about $10,000,000 of which about $1,000,000 was also given to various charitable purposes.

His life was so correct and his habits so regular that he uniformly enjoyed good health. His physical activity was undiminished and his mental faculties unimpaired, almost to the last, his death being due rather to the debility attending old age than to any acute or well defined disease. I had the privilege of seeing him the day before he died when although physically feeble, his mind had all its original brightness. After expressing his pleasure with the action of the Trustees in the selection of the site for the School and saying he hoped to meet them in a day or two, he said with much earnestness :

" Be sure to get from the Railroad Company all the rights and privileges you are entitled to for locating the School on the line of the road."

This the last business act of his life was characteristic of the man.

In a few hours he sank into unconsciousness from which he never rallied, and on the next day, March 7th, 1889, his long, honorable and useful life peacefully closed.

The ceremony of the day would be incomplete without the expression of some thoughts more strictly applicable to you, the boys composing this School for whose welfare in life its generous founder gave his means in so liberal measure, and which the Trustees selected by him for that purpose, have endeavored to put into practical form to the best of their ability, for your comfort, improvement and benefit. If I. V. Williamson had in his many-sided nature, one characteristic that dominated all others, it was his industry, his love of labor. He worked indefatigably up to the last days of his long, useful and honorable life of eighty-six years, and I am speaking his sentiments when I say to you that labor, earnest, persistent and continuous labor, in all its forms professional, artistic, industrial, manual and even menial, whether in field or forum, in camp or court, in office or counting house, on the scaffold or at the work bench, on the highway or in the mine, is not only essential to success but when faithfully performed and for useful purposes, is in the sight of sensible people always respectable. The hod carrier honest, sober and industrious in his humble calling, clad in his rough attire, is a more attractive personage, a more useful member of society, more entitled to its favorable regard than the accomplished idler, the corrupt politician, the dishonest speculator or the thieving bank wrecker who may wear more showy garments and display a more polished manner and a higher mental culture.

That man who starting in life from obscure or unknown parentage and the hut of poverty as his birth-place, struggling against and overcoming difficulties and surmounting oppositions, finally attains distinction in any useful occupation, is deservedly entitled to the respect of the community in which he lives and of which he forms an important part. The world's history shows that its greatest heroes and benefactors have been the self-made men, who

have fought their hard fight of success from poverty and
obscurity to positions of usefulness and distinction. Where
can be found a character more estimable in all that makes
true greatness than that eminent son of toil, Abraham
Lincoln, whose pure and noble life was so tragically ended
before his great work of reconstructing the Union which he
had saved was entered upon, and of whose coming and
career, America's Poet-artist, T. Buchanan Read (another
self-made man) prophesied in his greatest Poem "The New
Pastoral," written and published years before the name of
Abraham Lincoln was known outside of Springfield, in the
following remarkable lines, the scene of which was laid in
the then wilderness of Illinois :

> " Here the great statesman from the ranks of toil
> Shall rise, with judgment clear, as strong ~~and~~ as wise ;
> And, with a well directed patriot blow,
> Re-clinch the rivets in our Union bands,
> Which tinkering knaves have striven to set ajar,"

and whom another American Poet, Lowell, describes as the
" New birth of our new soil ; the first American."

Or that poor printer's boy of Boston who made his way to
the then village of Philadelphia and walked its streets with
his bundle of clothes under one arm and a loaf of bread
under the other, hunting a night's lodging and by hard,
persistent work became the renowned scientist, statesman,
patriot and philosopher, Benjamin Franklin.

Samuel Smiles, an English writer of much experience,
in his book called "Self Help," after quoting from J. Stuart
Mill the following sentiment, "The worth of a state in the
long run, is the worth of the individuals composing it," and

from Schiller the following doctrine that "the education of the human race consists in action, conduct, self-culture and self-control, all that disciplines a man and fits him for the proper performance of his duties and business of life," and from Bacon that "self-reliance and self-denial will teach a man to drink out of his own cistern and to eat his own sweet bread, and to learn and labor truly to get his living, and carefully to expend the good things committed to his trust" says, "By labor the earth has been subdued and man redeemed from barbarism ; nor has a single step been made in civilization without it. Labor is not only a necessity and a duty, but a blessing ; only the idler feels it to be a curse. The duty of work is written on the thews and muscles of the limbs, the mechanism of the hand, the nerves and lobes of the brain—the sum of whose healthy action is satisfaction and enjoyment. In the school of labor is taught the best practical wisdom ; nor is a life of manual employment incompatible with high mental culture," and cites many instances of men rising, by the force of their own efforts, from obscurity and poverty, to positions of great usefulness and distinction and among them the following ; "From the barber shop came Jeremy Taylor, the eminent preacher ; Sir Richard Arkwright, the inventor of the spinning Jenny ; Lord Tenterden, one of England's distinguished chief justices, and Turner the greatest among modern landscape painters.

Shakespeare, the greatest poetical genius the world has

ever produced, sprang from an obscure origin, his father being a butcher and he a wool comber.

John Milton was the son of a scrivener.

From the lowest class of day laborers arose such men as Brindley the engineer ; Cook the Navigator and Burns the poet.

From the trade of brick laying and masonry came Ben. Johnson, the author ; Edwards and Telford, the engineers; Hugh Miller, the geologist and Allen Cunningham, the poet and sculptor ; while from the carpenter's work bench sprang Inigo Jones, the architect ; Harrison, the chronometer maker; John Hunter, the physiologist; Romney and Opie the painters; Professor Lee, the orientalist and John Gibson, the sculptor.

The weavers have produced Simson, the mathematician ; Bacon, the sculptor ; the two Milners, Adam Walker, John Foster, Jacquard, Wilson the ornithologist, Dr. Livingstone, the missionary traveller ; Joseph Brotherton and Fox distinguished members of Parliament.

Shoemakers have produced Admiral Sir Cloudesly Shovel ; Sturgeon, the electrician ; Samuel Drew, the essayist ; Gifford, the editor of "The Quarterly Review ;" Bloomfield, the Poet ; and Thomas Edwards, the naturalist.

Tailors have been distinguished in the person of John Stow, the historian ; Sir John Hawkson, Admiral Hobson, and in one of our Presidents, Andrew Johnson.

Cardinal Wolsey, DeFoe, Akenside and Kirk White, were sons of butchers, Bunyan was a tinker and Joseph Lancaster a basket maker, and Richard Cobden's start in life was equally obscure.

Among the greatest names identified with the invention of the steam engine were the mechanics Newcomen, a blacksmith ; Watts, a maker of mathematical instruments, and Stephenson, an engine fireman.

Herschel played in a military band, Chantrey was a wood carver, Sir Thomas Lawrence was the son of a tavern keeper, Sir Humphrey Davy an apothecary's apprentice, and Michael Faraday the son of a blacksmith, was a book binder.

Among those who have given the greatest impulse to the sublime science of astronomy we find Copernicus, the son of a Polish baker ; Kepler, the son of a German innkeeper and himself a waiter at the tables ; d'Alembert, a foundling ; Newton, the son of a farmer in a small way, and La Place, of a poor peasant.

After citing these and other instances of men who have surmounted great difficulties and obstacles in achieving distinction the same author (Smiles) says :

" In all these cases, strenuous individual application was the price paid for the distinction, excellence of any sort being invariably placed beyond the reach of indolence. It is the diligent hand and head alone that maketh rich in self culture, growth in wisdom and in business ; even when men are born to wealth and high social position, any solid reputation which they may individually achieve can only be attained by energetic application, for though an inheritance of acres may be bequeathed, an inheritance of knowledge and wisdom cannot. The wealthy man may pay others for doing his work for him, but it is impossible to get his thinking done for him by another or to purchase any kind of self culture."

Citing as conspicuous instances of men whose lives although being under more favorable surroundings were diligently and continuously devoted to hard work as essential to success, such names as Bacon, Worcester, Boyle, Cavandish, Talbot and Rosse in philosophy and science; Sir Robert Peel, Brougham, Palmerston, Derby, Russell, D'Israeli and Gladstone as statesmen; Scott, Dickens, Thackery and others in literature who were always too busy to think of observing any eight or ten hours laws for regulating their labors, and concludes one of his chapters as follows:

" In fine, human character is moulded by a thousand subtle influences; by example and precept; by life and literature; by friends and neighbors; by the world we live in as well as by the spirits of our forefathers, whose legacy of good words and deeds we inherit. But great, unquestionably, though these influences are acknowledged to be, it is nevertheless equally clear that men must necessarily be the active agents of their own well being and well doing; and that however much the wise and the good may owe to others, they themselves must in the very nature of things be their own best helpers."

The above instances of distinguished self-made men, whose start in life was not equal to that now furnished to you in this well equipped school, were and are of the English or other foreign races, with whom the opportunities for achieving such distinction are less favorable than those prevailing in this free republic which has produced many such illustrious names.

In addition to Franklin and Lincoln, of whom special mention has been made, the Revolutionary period of our history gave us Washington, .the surveyor; Greene, the blacksmith; Putnam and Wayne (the farmer boys), in war;

Robert Morris in finance; the Adams', Patrick Henry, Otis, Hamilton, Madison, Jay and Jefferson in Statesmanship, and Charles Thompson, principal of a Friends' Academy, the patriot scholar of the Revolution, Secretary of the American Congress for fifteen years, learned writer and author of one of the best translations of the Bible, known among the Indians as "the man of truth," whom John Adams describes as "the Sam Adams of Philadelphia, the life of the cause of ~~the cause of~~ liberty " (who was also a Friend or Quaker, in all except actual membership in the society), and at a later period in its history, such names as Albert Gallatin in finance, Daniel Webster and Henry Clay in oratory and statesmanship, and Andrew Jackson and Millard Fillmore (originally a mill operative), and coming down to more recent times, such champions of freedom as Phillips and Garrison, Lovejoy and Greely, Beecher and Sumner, Wilmot, Stevens, Kelley (originally a jeweler's apprentice), and Garfield, (originally a canal boatman), and in the war for the preservation of the Union, such heroes and patriots as Grant, the soldier, statesman and patriot, who in a few short strides and solely upon the strength of his own merit, passed from the tan yard to the head of the largest and grandest army the world has ever seen, and by his bravery, wisdom and fidelity to duty, saved his country from ruin, and of whom President Harrison when recently standing in the room in which he died, at Mt. McGregor, said, in his apt and sententious phrase, "The life of a man so great as was General Grant does not go *out*, it goes *on*," and his able Lieutenants, Sherman and

Sheridan, and Meade and Thomas, and Hancock and a host of others distinguished for bravery, skill and patriotism.

In law and literature, such names as Marshall, Story, Kent and Sharswood, Carey, Bancroft, Cooper, Longfellow, Hawthorne, Bayard Taylor, Whittier and Lowell; and in science, mechanics, invention and useful industries, such names as Fulton and Fitch, Oliver Evans and Eli Whitney, Professors Henry, Morse, Barker and Leidy, and Erickson, Edison, Baldwin, Howe and Hoe. And in the accumulation of large fortunes honestly acquired by lives of patient industry and devoted to purposes of education, the relief of suffering humanity in all its various forms and many channels of practical benevolence, such honored names as Stephen Girard, I. V. Williamson, George Peabody, Johns Hopkins, Asa Packer and Peter Cooper, who have passed on to their reward, and such living examples of the same virtues as our own Anthony J. Drexel and George W. Childs, and Enoch Pratt and Jacob Tome, of our neighboring sister state of Maryland.

You are born to a goodly heritage. You have come into this world when it has reached an age of wonderful activities and marvellous material development in all directions; not merely to play a part in its performances or to enjoy its pleasures, but to discharge its duties and realize its responsibilities.

You are citizens of a free republic with a territory of vast extent washed on either side by the two great oceans of the world, embracing every variety of soil and climate, a land whose surface is large enough in area and rich enough in soil to raise crops sufficient to feed the whole human race, and underlaid with a mineral wealth beyond the power of figures to compute—a republic in which every man is a sovereign, the equal in the eye of the law of every other man and having an equal voice in the making of the laws to which all are subject—a country in which there is not only no interference by law with a proper and healthy competition among workmen for superiority or supremacy, but whose laws are so administered as to encourage every workman to excel his associates by greater industry or better knowledge.

The only impediment to such deserved distinction as attends superior merit, is to be found in such practices as destroy the incentive of the individual to reach the highest standard by the cultivation of industry, sobriety and integrity, in fixing the compensation for all workmen, the efficient and inefficient alike at the same rigid figure.

The census of 1890 recently published shows that your country has a population exceeding 62,000,000 and an assessed valuation of $24,000,000,000 (Twenty-four thousand million of dollars) of property and according to the usual recognized and admitted difference between assessments for taxation and actual values, these figures indicate an aggregate national wealth of $62,000,000,000 (Sixty-two thousand millions) an average of $1,000 to each man, woman and child. These official statistics prove the United States to be by $12,000,000,000 the richest country in the world exceeding Great Britain, which had previously been the first, by $12,000,000,000 and France by $16,000,000,000. The actual increase in wealth during the last decade from 1880 to 1890 being $18,000,000,000, a sum larger than the whole aggregate wealth of the country in 1860 which then represented the accumulations of seventy years. The per capita share twice what it was in 1860, one-third larger than in 1870 and one-fifth larger than in 1880. A country which within the last twenty-five years has reduced its national debt from $2,758,000,000 to $977,000,000, and in ten years from 1880 to 1890 has added $2,000,000,000 to its capital invested in manufactures alone, an increase of nearly 75 per cent., and in the same time increasing the annual value of its manufactured products from $5,300,000,000 to $8,600,000,000 or in other words producing manufactured goods at the rate of $3,300,000,000 a year above the products of ten years ago. The increase in capital invested in manufacturing within the last ten years is greater than the entire amount of capital invested in that industry only twenty years ago. And in the same period of ten years this country has built 73,500 miles of rail road, almost as much as the total mileage of 1880, at a cost for construction and equipment of $4,030,000,000.

In regard to gold and silver coin and bullion and paper money secured by and redeemed in coin, regarded as one of the most positive and reliable tests of the actual wealth of a nation and indicative of the legitimate demands of business, it may be stated from official sources that the aggregate on

July 1st, 1880, was $1,205,929.17, being $19.41 per capita of population, and on July 1st, 1891, these figures had been increased to $2,100,130,092, being $23.45 per capita.

As compared with foreign leading commercial nations the following statement is made as to gold and silver coin and bullion carried by the representative financial institutions on October 1st, 1891: The Bank of England held $125,000,000: the Bank of Germany, $225,000,000; the Bank of France, $515,000,000 and the United States Treasury and National Banks together held $845,000,000,000.

The number of patents issued for useful inventions up to 1880 was 223,211, and from 1880 to 1890 there were issued 195,454, and the aggregate up to October 1st, 1891, is 460,545.

A country whose crop for the present year alone (1891) of what is known as cereal productions, used as food such as wheat, corn, rye and barley (apart from other productions of immense value such as cotton, hay, fruits, oil, metals and domestic animals) has amounted to 1,000,000,000 of bushels having an actual market value at present prices of $1,732,000,000 about $500,000,000 more than that of last year.

And in this same year 1891 nearly $75,000,000 in gold has been furnished by the United States to Europe upon a sudden call to that effect to relieve its bankers and capitalists from financial embarrassments, and another $100,000,000 it is estimated have been sent abroad to meet the expenditures made by American tourists and pleasure seekers, and all this immense exportation of the gold of the country without producing any serious disturbance of its financial condition.

No other nation shows such a growth in population or material wealth and progress ; and in this connection it may be remarked, if incidentally, with perfect propriety and entire truthfulness, that during these years of unexampled prosperity and increase, the policy of the general government has been steadily in the direction of protection to American labor and fostering of American industries under what is known as the protective tariff system of imposing duties on foreign imports.

The responsive assent from this large and intelligent audience to the truism expressed in the above paragraph, induces me to add that the Board of Trustees of this School as now constituted propose to teach as part of its course of instruction, three great principles, viz : patriotism, protection and piety, but not in a partisan or political spirit,—a patriotism which shall be national not sectional, a protection which shall be general and reciprocal, not special or limited, and a piety which shall be pure and practical and free from sectarian bias, as these were the principles which I. V. Williamson believed in and practised.

You are a part of this great nation—you are to assist in keeping up and increasing its prosperity, and maintaining its character in the family of nations.

Your success or failure in life is to a large extent in your own hands. It was the design and purpose of I. V. Williamson, and it is the intention of the trustees charged with the duty of administering the trust committed to them, to furnish you with all the means, facilities and inducements to make your lives successful. The Trustees of this school, with its President, Superintendent, corps of teachers and all other employees will endeavor to do their full duty to you in their respective positions as managers, instructors and caretakers, and they ask in return that you will do the same in your position as scholars—that you will be respectful to them and obedient to rules, that you will be diligent in the school-room, and industrious in the work-shop, judicious in your amusements and recreation (for which ample time will be allowed you), correct in your habits, courteous in manner and unselfish in conduct to each other, pure in thought, . chaste in speech, and above all, honorable and upright in sentiment and feeling, and truthful both in act and language.

They also ask that when you have finished your course of three years, more or less, in this school, and leave its walls with a certificate of proficiency in your various trades, that you will carry into your daily lives, and manifest by your actions the results of your tuition and training here. That you will feel an honorable pride in your respective callings, that you will make your employer's interests your own— work for him and with him as if for yourselves—that you will show readiness to do not only your allotted tasks, but a willingness to go beyond them, and thus insure your success by making yourselves so indispensable to him as to compel him to realize that he cannot do without you, and thus command your own terms as to wages.

You are all now at the most impressionable period of your lives, just at that age when character is forming, and it is reasonably certain that the lessons here learned, the habits here formed, the principles of thought and action here acquired, will mould and determine your future careers.

"In morals as well as in mathematics the straight line is the shortest distance between two points." Try to walk this straight, short line ; strive to be direct and honest in all things. Love *Truth* with a deep and absorbing passion. Make the observance of it the rule of your lives, avoiding even the slightest approach to falsehood and deception. This is the corner-stone and foundation upon which alone can be erected that structure in the moral being, known as character, which rests upon and grows out of correct principles and pure thoughts, producing good acts and making a useful, noble life, which is in itself a living truth.

> "This above all : to thine own self be true,
> And it must follow as the night the day,
> Thou cans't not then be false to any man."

In a recently published article from the pen of the accomplished John Russell Young, giving some reminiscences of that distinguished statesman and patriot, Hamilton Fish, who still lives full of years and honors, chief among which is that of having been for eight years the trusted personal friend and confidential official adviser of General Grant while President, he was asked by Mr. Young what he considered the dominant quality of Grant's nature, and he replied at once and with emphasis, "absolute truthfulness, complete, inflexible veracity." So that great as was General Grant in his courage, in his military genius, in his sagacity, his magnanimity, his knowledge of men and affairs, the greatest of all his great qualities was his love for and devotion to pure and absolute truthfulness.

All that has been said to you on this subject has been well condensed in some sound and sensible advice given to the scholars in Girard College by one of its directors, himself a living example of what can be accomplished by a life of purity, truthfulness and uprightness, unselfishly devoted to good work. This good man and useful citizen, trusted and honored by the community in which he lives and labors as few men have been, who, although born of a distinguished family, was poor in this world's goods, beginning his business career in the lowest position in a store, has by the cultivation and practice of the principles to which reference has been made, risen to the distinction of being one of the most eminent bankers and financial authorities in the land. In one of the excellent addresses made by him to the pupils of the College he says :

"I say then to you boys, do your best ; be honest and diligent, be resolute to live a pure and honorable life, speak the truth like boys who hope to be gentlemen, be merry if you will, for it is good to be merry and wise, be loving and dutiful sons, be affectionate brothers, be loyal hearted friends and when you come to be men you will look back to these boyish days without regret and without shame.

"Something like this is my ideal of a boy. I am very desirous that your future shall be bright and useful and successful, and I, and others who are interested in your welfare, will hope to hear nothing but good of you ; but we can have no greater joy than to hear that you are walking in the truth. Some of you may become rich men, some may become very prominent in public affairs : and reach high places ; you may fill a large space in the public estimation ;

you may be able and brilliant men, but there is nothing in your life that will give us so much joy as to hear that you are walking in the truth.''

'' Truth is the foundation of all the virtues, and without it reputation is absolutely worthless. No gentleness of disposition, no willingness to help other people, no habits of industry can make up for want of truthfulness of heart and life. Some persons think that if they work long and hard, and deny themselves for the good of others, and do many generous and noble acts, and have a good reputation, they can even tell lies sometimes and not be much blamed. But they forget that reputation is not character; that one may have a very good reputation and a very bad character, they forget that the reputation is the outside, what we see of each other, while the character is what we are in heart.''

There can be no more fitting conclusion to this address than the expression of the wish that you will all take to heart and profit by these words of sound wisdom and fatherly affection.

MR. HUEY said:

The Trustees of the Williamson School are profoundly grateful to the other educational institutions of this country for their kindly sympathy and assistance while we have been deliberating and building. They early gave us to understand that any information in their power to give was at our service, and that they would esteem it a favor if we would call upon them freely for the results of their experience. One of the most prominent of these, the University of Pennsylvania, further testifies its interest in us by sending one of its most eminent professors, who promptly responded to our invitation that he should address us this afternoon. It is with much pleasure that I introduce to you Professor George F. Barker, of the University of Pennsylvania.

Address by Professor George F. Barker, of the University of Pennsylvania.

I do not quite understand why, save by the kind partiality of my friend Mr. Townsend, I should have been asked to say a word upon this interesting occasion, unless, perhaps, for the reason that a portion of my early life was spent in the workshop, and that in consequence of this apprenticeship, I have a warm sympathy with my young friends before me who have just entered the Williamson Free School of Mechanical Trades to fit themselves for the work of life.

I should not be true to my own feelings therefore, if I did not respond to this invitation and say this word to-day. If I did not avail myself of this opportunity to express, in the first place, my gratification at what I see here, and to rejoice, not only in the benevolence of Mr. Williamson, but also at the highly satisfactory way in which the Trustees have carried his intention into effect, and, aided by President Shrigley and Superintendent Crawford, have provided these excellently arranged and well equipped buildings. If I did not also express the cordial good wishes of the great University with which I am connected, for the success of this movement for the education of the hand as well as the head. If, finally, I did not say what I could to assist and encourage you who are taking to-day the most important step of your lives.

With you, I have listened with great pleasure to the admirable address of Mr. Townsend. So complete is it that I feel, that in speaking to you, I can hardly do more than echo his words of advice and counsel. At such a time as this the thought involuntarily arises ; what are the results that should be obtained in such an Institution as this, endowed so liberally and furnished so abundantly with all the appliances needed to carry on its work ? Education, it should ever be remembered, is the development of the student's powers by his own exertions. The most competent instructors, the best machines and tools, no matter how liberally provided, can aid the work only by furnishing opportunities. To attain the coveted championship, the athlete must himself enter upon a course of training, and must develope his muscle solely by his own exercise of them. The same is true of education. Physiologists tell us that in the brain there are cells of gray matter in which all mental and nervous power originates. Some of these cells are devoted to the control of muscular action ; others to the production of thought. The education of these cells is a process which consists simply of a repetition upon them of impressions from without. By these repeated impressions, the cell is modified in its structure and *residua* are left within it, in virtue of which it responds more and more promptly with each repetition, and reproduces more exactly the originating impressions. How slow and irregular for example are the motions of a child when it is learning to walk ; how uncertain at first are the movements of the hands, when a beginner is learning to play the piano. But as, by repetition the cells concerned in these actions become educated, the required operations are performed, not only certainly and rapidly, but often automatically and without conscious effort.

Perhaps it will be useful for us to-day to consider a little more, at length, the difference between thought-cells and motor-cells. Thought-cells are concerned in purely mental operations; they enable us to think and to reason. Motorcells furnish the impulses by which muscular actions are originated, and motions of the body or its parts are performed. Hitherto in the past, education has consisted mainly in producing impressions upon the thought-cells and in organizing *residua* in them. This operation constitutes the intellectual education of the college and the university.

In these latter days, however, the motor-cells are claiming a share in the educational movement. Hence, industrial schools have arisen, the object of which is to train these motor-cells that the responses, both muscular and sensorial, which they make to the calls upon them, shall be prompt and effective.

But this is only a portion of the truth. Precisely as in intellectual education it is found desirable to some extent also to train the sense to perceive and the hands to execute, so on the other hand industrial education, intelligence in the use of mechanical appliances, requires a collateral education of the intellect. It is in the intelligence of the American Mechanic that this superiority lies. Hence, as I understand the matter it is the object of this Williamson School to teach the students who come within its walls, the intelligent use of tools.

The practical man of to-day, however, must do more than execute. He must originate. He must not only do work which others have done before him and do it better than they have done it, but he must devise and solve new problems never before considered—he must contrive new and better methods of producing desirable results. Now, it is in the thought cells that the faculty of originality resides and hence the power to invent new devices and to supply new methods results from education of the intelligence. His value as an employee it may be, lies in his power to execute : but his value to the community as a mechanician lies in his power to originate. True the genius of invention is often tardily recognized and at the outset at least goes unrewarded. Edison as a telegraph operator, was easily among the first in his calling, but his originality and fertility in invention which have now made him the foremost inventor of the day, cost him more than once his position as an operator. That eminent Philadelphian, Joseph Saxton, whom Professor Bache pronounced "the greatest mechanical genius the world ever saw" and who finally attained to the honor of membership in the National Academy of Sciences, was for many years unrecognized. Although he made the clock which now keeps time in the tower of Independence Hall, yet it was in London that he subsequently made the first magneto-electric machine and obtained the first magneto-electric spark. He was recalled from Europe to build the first machinery of the Philadelphia Mint and he constructed the dies which were used at that Mint during seven years, and was finally appointed Superintendent of Weights and Measures in the United States Coast Survey in Washington. There he constructed the Government standards and made a balance which would weigh to a three-millionth part of its load. James Watt, the illustrious inventor of the steam engine, when only six years old, was observed one day drawing all sorts of lines on the floor with a piece of chalk—a friend of his father's remonstrated, saying "Why do you allow that boy to waste his time. Send him to the public school," before you criticise, replied his father, "examine what he is doing." It turned out that he was attempting the solution of a problem in geometry. Even at the age of fourteen his grandmother said to him, " I never saw such an idle boy as you are. Do take a book and employ yourself usefully, upwards of a half an hour has elapsed without your saying a single word. Do you know what you have been doing all this time ? You have taken off and replaced and taken off again the tea pot lid, and you have alternately held in the steam that came out, first a saucer and then a spoon, you have busied yourself in examining and collecting together the little drops formed by the condensation of the steam on the surface of the china and of the silver ; is it not disgraceful to waste your time in this manner?" and yet out of these simple experiments, by which the boy was educating his thought cells, came that wonderful machinery which has done as much to advance civilization as any device invented by man. Herodotus tells us that to build the Great Pyramid required the work of 100,000 men for twenty years. By the aid of one of the immense steam engines now in common use in our ocean steamers a single man could complete this amount of work in six weeks.

It may perhaps appear to you that I have not been fortunate in my selection of illustrious examples, since neither Watt nor Saxton, nor Edison ever had more than a few months of education, and that only in the common school. But I have mentioned these names advisedly. They attained their high positions in the world in spite of their early disadvantages. Watt, owing to feeble health, and Saxton and Edison because of limited means, were not able to avail themselves of the education of the schools. Because of the great power given to them by Nature, which enabled them to train their thought-cells, themselves unaided by outside appliances, they were able to achieve success. No such success is possible without this cell education. It may be obtained by laborious self-study without assistance, or it may be obtained by the use of all available appliances. Great as many men have become who have educated themselves, it is impossible now to believe that they might have been even greater had the helps of the world also been available and availed of. Hence, the wisdom of creating schools for the education of the eye and the hand as well as the mind. In this Williamson School the Watts, and Saxtons, and Edisons of to-day can find the education they desire, and more than all, can find it at a price they can all afford to pay.

The object of education then, my young friends, is to improve the natural talents with which you are endowed. To do this, you must avail yourselves of every opportunity to exert upon the brain-cells those impressions which you are likely to want in your life-work, either as such or as constituent elements in the new combinations you desire to produce. In future years you are likely to have splendid opportunities offered you to make both reputation and fortune. How unfortunate would it be, if when you seek in the brain-cells for the stored knowledge necessary to enable you to utilize these opportunities, you should find these cells empty, through neglect of the educational facilities here supplied to you. Like Mother Hubbard, you find the cupboard bare and disastrous consequences follow. Let me urge you then to make every use of the opportunities here offered. Believe your instructors when they assure you that everything which you are taught in this school will have important applications in your future life. Some years ago a writer in the British Quarterly Review made the statement that a bar of iron costing but one pound sterling could be made into horse shoes worth two and a half pounds, into table knives worth thirty-six pounds, into needles worth seventy-one pounds, into penknife blades worth six hundred and ninety-seven pounds, or into the balance springs of watches worth fifty thousand pounds. But iron is passive and can only be worked upon. You are active and must do yourselves the work of education which is needed to increase your value. You are in every sense the arbiters of your own fortunes. You alone can say whether you shall be worth to the generation in which you live fifty thousand times as much as you were when you entered the Williamson School, or whether you shall be worth only two and a half times as much. Which shall it be?

At the conclusion of the address MR. HUEY said:

With the permission of the audience the students will now retire, and thirty-five of them will go at once to the workshop and take their places at their benches. After they have left the room the friends present are invited and urged to make a thorough examination of the grounds and buildings, and to inspect the shops in so far as they are equipped. Everything is open to you and we trust that you will avail yourselves of this opportunity to become thoroughly acquainted with what is being done here, and appreciate the kindly thought of the man who made this School a possibility.

MR. TOWNSEND addressing the boys, then said:

You and we are honored by the presence on this platform of one of the original Trustees of this School, who in its organization and early working gave faithful and intelligent attention to the duties of the position until he was called to a higher plane and wider field of action, in which he is serving the country with signal ability and usefulness. He too, is another conspicuous example of a self made man. His start in life was as an office boy upon a very slender salary, but by the exercise of the qualities referred to in the address to which you have listened, he has achieved an enviable distinction. He has been known to the community in which he has lived and labored for more than thirty years as an upright, successful merchant and consistent Christian, and in later years has achieved a national fame as an intelligent, indefatigable and honest cabinet minister. He was a near and valued friend of the founder of this school. His good heart is always with us, and, although 'a very busy public man, he is with us here to-day to show his interest in our work. I take great pleasure in introducing to you Postmaster General John Wanamaker, who spoke as follows :

ADDRESS OF HON. JOHN WANAMAKER.

Mr. President,—

I respond at your command, though I was not appointed to speak to-day. The speakers who have preceded me have therefore had the advantage of me and I am without a manuscript or any notes. But my whole heart is beating so fast with its old love for the little, quiet Quaker man, whose face looks down from the wall upon us, that I must give expression to my sense of gratitude for this great benefaction he has spread around and over these boys who are henceforth his children. We who are guardians are but stepfathers. He was, and is, the real great hearted father whose memory will brighten as the years roll on.

In your admirable address, Mr. Chairman of the Board, you spoke of him as a country boy, doing the usual boy's work about the farm. I wonder if he ever planted a tree ? Among all the country boys that ever blessed our city, by their examples of diligence, uprightness and usefulness, which of them all ever planted such a tree as this, the fruit of which, will, in all the ages to come, be shelter, education and inspiration to thousands of the boys of Pennsylvania.

You fine fellows who have been honored to be the first on the roll and who are to head the procession and set the copy by your endeavors and successes, for the long line of boys that are to follow, are fortunate in not having been born too soon. By the use you make of your opportunity will the influence of not only your lives, but of this long thought of and carefully planned school, be felt throughout the land.

One day, in New York, when the Cooper Institute was in course of completion, there came in to one of the rooms, where painters were at work at a ceiling, an old man wearing a slouch hat, to whom the painters called, "Say, old man, will you steady this scaffold a little, while we finish the work up here?" and the old man quickly took hold of the ladders on which they stood and kept them from falling while they worked. That old man, though they knew it not, was Peter Cooper, the philanthropist, who was putting his money into that great building which was to be a great scaffold on which young men were to stand while they worked hard to get an education for their life work. When was it that Peter Cooper would'nt lend a hand when he could help his fellow-men?

This building and the others that cluster about it and still more to come shall be the scaffolding that Isaiah V. Williamson will hold up for boys to put unfading color and character upon their lives. While our benefactor lived, there were some who looked upon him walking the streets, to and from his little office, clad in old fashioned, well worn, but well kept clothes, who said that he was a mean man ; but to-day you see by all these signs about you what kind of meanness it was that animated his life. He saved his money that he might save boys, who would need an education, that he once knew the need of himself.

Down along the Potomac River, twenty miles below Washington, at Indian Head, at this very hour, the Secretary of the Navy and many scientific men are engaged in testing the nickel-plate armor, intended to encase the battle-ships of the Government. Some of our gentle hearted, peace loving Quaker friends, may think our Nation does not need war ships, but it may be handy to have them around, whenever our foreign relations grow in any way "chilly." The experiments with the armor are to ascertain how far it will resist our great guns, that throw cannon balls against it. The results of these tests of armor will be watched all over the world, and so this becomes a doubly historic day, by the additional event of the opening of this Industrial School, intended to project against this world, in days to come, forces of the most tremendous power, to promote its peace and order.

You are the great guns to be loaded in this magazine with the powers of cultivated minds, trained eyes, skilled hands and uplooking hearts, by which your well rounded lives will be irresistable when you come in connection with the world. The greatest want of this age is men. Pennsylvania has never been wanting in some such like Matthew Baldwin, John Welsh and I. V. Williamson, but she does wisely in planting here some of her best boys, that they may grow into the right kind of men. But the making of a good man requires a good boy ; an idle, careless, wasteful boy is not likely to be much of a man. The last thing that I think my old friend, Mr. Williamson, would care to do, would be to waste a thousand dollars on a ten cent boy, trying the impossible thing of making a man out of him.

We are your friends to help you all we can, but your chief help must, under God, be yourselves. You shall not lack for cheer and counsel. The Chairman of the Board of Trustees, whose wise words to-day, I trust, will be printed, that each boy who comes into the school, may know its history and its aims, will always be your sympathizing, true friend. Mr. Cummins, who of all others was possibly the nearest friend of Mr. Williamson, is deeply interested in you and his friendship is worth your having. Whenever you see him, take off your hats to him, as you would to the founder of this school. And now, then, in conclusion of this already long, impromptu speech, in the evening of this beautiful Indian Summer day, I charge you, young men of the school, entering upon a new era of your lives, to so use these recitation halls and workshops, that your industry and high resolves, while you strive together here, may be to you all, the sunrise of noble lives.

Mr. Huey :

We hoped to have with us to-day Col. Richard T. Auchmuty, founder and principal of the New York Trades

School, who was the pioneer and is a successful leader in the work in which we are interested, but being unable to be present in person, he has sent the following letter :

LENOX, MASS., October 23d, 1891.

PRESIDENT JOHN M. SHRIGLEY,

DEAR SIR :—I regret that it will not be possible for me to avail myself of the kind invitation of the Trustees and Officers of the Williamson Free School of Mechanical Trades, to be present and make an address at the opening exercises on Saturday, October 31st.

May all of us who have undertaken the training of our young countrymen in the mechanical art, remember that this country not only needs and can have the best skilled workmen in the world, but that it also needs workmen who will be good citizens, loyal to our institutions and believing in American ideas of liberty and justice.

Yours very truly,

RICHARD T. AUCHMUTY.